Collegevi

THE MINISTRY OF COMMUNION

Second Edition

Michael Kwatera, O.S.B.

LITURGICAL PRESS
Collegeville, Minnesota

www.litpress.org

Dedicated to
the extraordinary ministers of Holy Communion
who serve the Church
in the Diocese of St. Cloud, Minnesota

Design by Joachim Rhoades, O.S.B. Photography: cover image by Gene Plaisted, O.S.C.; interior images by W. P. Wittman Photography Limited.

1	2	3	4	5	6	7	8

Library of Congress Cataloging-in-Publication Data

Kwatera, Michael.
  The ministry of Communion / Michael Kwatera.—2nd ed.
    p. cm. — (Collegeville ministry series)
  Includes bibliographical references.
  ISBN 0-8146-2958-X (pbk : alk. paper)
    1. Lord's Supper—Catholic Church.   I. Title.   II. Series.
BX2235.K85   2004
264'.02036—dc22   2004004303

Contents

Preface   v

1. Being and Giving the Body of Christ:
   A Life of Ministry   1

2. Being and Giving the Body of Christ:
   Practical Suggestions   7

   Ministry of Communion
   within the Assembly   9
       Sharing the Bread   14
       Sharing the Cup   16

   Ministry of Communion
   to the Sick and Homebound   21

3. Lay-Led Communion Services   26

4. Looking for the Perfect Eucharistic Minister   34

Notes   38

Act of Personal Recommitment
for Extraordinary Ministers of Holy Communion   40

Preface

This booklet is offered to people who are known by various names: "extraordinary ministers of Holy Communion"— "eucharistic ministers"—"Communion ministers." These persons, whatever their title, have become an indispensable part of the ministry of Communion in parishes, hospitals, and religious communities.

You have accepted a share in this ministry. No matter where you exercise it, you are not a Communion *distributor* (a distributor is part of an automobile engine's electrical system or a person in marketing!). You are a *minister* of Communion, a title that clearly identifies you as one who serves God's holy people.

Pope Paul VI explained the need for your service in his Instruction on Facilitating Sacramental Eucharistic Communion in Particular Circumstances (1973), where he described how a lack of sufficient clergy for the sharing of Communion could occur:

> During Mass, because of the size of the congregation or a particular difficulty in which a celebrant finds himself; outside of Mass, when it is difficult because of distance to take the sacred species, especially in the Viaticum, to the sick in danger of death, or when the very number of the sick, especially in hospitals and similar institutions, requires many ministers.[1]

With these circumstances in mind, Paul VI authorized extraordinary ministers of Holy Communion to share the Body and Blood of Christ with their fellow worshipers in the assembly and with those confined to their homes, so that no one "be deprived of this sacramental help and consolation."[2]

The exhortations of Pope Pius X for frequent and early Communion (1905, 1910) have resulted in an unprecedented number of Christians receiving Communion at each Mass. Extraordinary ministers of Holy Communion render valuable service in places where "the number of faithful requesting Holy Communion is such that the celebration of Mass or the distribution of the Eucharist outside of Mass would be unduly prolonged."[3] As an extraordinary minister of Holy Communion, you help ensure that the Communion rite of the eucharistic celebration, important though it be, not be disproportionately long in relation to the other parts. Your ministry also enables a congregation to share in Communion services when a priest cannot be present for the celebration of the Eucharist.

In the past, the scarcity of priests, deacons, and acolytes may have caused the sick and those confined to their homes to be deprived of the Eucharist for long periods of time. Now, through your ministry, they are able to receive their saving Lord in Communion more frequently.

In 1978 the bishops of the United States voted to extend permission for the congregation to receive both the bread and the wine at Sunday and holy day Masses. This welcome practice has increased the need for extraordinary ministers in the sharing of Communion, and it will continue to do so. It is probable that in the United States, at the present time, more Sunday communicants receive the Eucharist from the hands of extraordinary ministers than from clergy. The desirable and significant role of lay persons in the ministry of Communion is here to stay!

Your ministry complements and extends the ministry of the clergy. Yet your ministry is not only that of "official assistant" to the clergy; it is a particular way of exercising your baptismal priesthood. You are among your fellow worshipers as one who serves; you cannot lose sight of your oneness with them, nor of your oneness with the priest celebrant as he serves the assembly in its worship. You also have a ministry to your fellow liturgical ministers: you are to share with them the joy and strength your service brings to you and so build them up in love. It is my hope that this booklet will deepen your joy and renew your strength in the ministry of Communion.

My comments and suggestions draw upon the excellent work in *Touchstones for Liturgical Ministers*, published jointly by The Liturgical Conference and The Federation of Diocesan Liturgical Commissions (1978).

Michael Kwatera, O.S.B.

Solemnity of the Most Holy Body and Blood of Christ
June 13, 2004

Being and Giving the Body of Christ
A Life of Ministry

For as in one body we have many parts, and all the parts do not have the same function, so we, though many, are one body in Christ and individually parts of one another. (Rom 12:4-5)

We easily think of the consecrated bread and wine of the Eucharist as something holy, as something filled with God's life—and rightly so. The Eucharist is the Body and Blood of Jesus Christ, the Son of God. Yet, in the Eucharist, God the Father likes to start with something that comes from us—with something *human*. God the Father starts with human food—bread and wine—and lets them become the Body and Blood of God's Son through the power of the Holy Spirit. God the Father lets us start with our bread—a symbol of all that nourishes our human life—and with our wine—a symbol of all that gladdens and saddens our human life—and lets us share the joys and sorrows of his Son as we eat and drink in his memory. The bread and wine that we place on the altar—human gifts of little material value—must be transformed by the Spirit of God to become the Body and Blood of Christ. Then we receive back our poor, human gifts as the richest gift of God's love: God's beloved Son.

In the Eucharist, God the Father starts with the *human*—the bread and wine on the altar, and the bread and wine of *our human lives*—and brings out the *beyond-the-human*, the *divine*, in them. Bread and wine, the work of human hands, become the Body and Blood of Christ. But the change doesn't end there: by sharing in the Body and Blood of Christ, *we become what we receive!* St. Augustine, the fifth-century bishop of Hippo in North Africa, preached about this marvel often, and had a yearly opportunity to explain it to those newly baptized at Easter: "Because He [the Lord] suffered for us, He left us in this Sacrament His Body and Blood, which He made even as He made us, also. For we have become His Body, and through His mercy we are what we receive."[4] To become a member of the Body of Christ through baptism is to take one's place in the intimate circle of God's worshipers, the family circle that we glimpse in an imaginary letter of St. Luke in Roger Lloyd's *The Letters of Luke the Physician*. Luke is describing a celebration of the Eucharist to a curious friend of his:

> You would look round casually at the worshippers, and they would seem to you very, very ordinary, and even mediocre. But all that would be because you were looking at it critically from the outside. No one can understand what it means to us unless

he is himself part and parcel of it, standing on the inside of the circle, and sharing in the deep experience of worshipping our Lord Jesus.[5]

Like St. Luke and St. Paul, St. Augustine believed that our sharing in the Eucharist changes us. Augustine repeated this belief often, lest his congregation forget that their sharing in the Body of Christ really formed them *into* the Body of Christ. "Behold what you have received!" he told them. "Therefore, just as you see that the bread which was made is one mass, so may you also be one Body by loving one another, by having one faith, one hope, and an undivided charity."[6] Such is the great dignity and responsibility of us who share in the Body and Blood of Christ: our lives are to affirm that the Body of Christ is one in faith, hope, and love, even though it has many members. And just in case there might be some people in Augustine's congregation who still hadn't got the point, he made a declaration that may startle us by its simple truthfulness: "There you are on the table, and there you are in the chalice."[7] We, though many, are members of the one Body of Christ; we are one with Christ our Head in the Eucharist. Through our human gifts of bread and wine and our very lives, and through the divine gift of the Father's beloved Son, we become what we receive in the Eucharist: the Body of Christ. This marvelous transformation is what the author of the song "To Be Your Bread" invites us to ask for humbly: "To be Your bread now, be Your wine now, Lord, come and change us, to be a Sign of Your love. Blest and broken, poured and flowing, gift that You gave us, to be Your body once again."[8]

For extraordinary ministers of Holy Communion, there is another dignity and responsibility: you must become what you *give*. You must *become* and *live* as the Body of Christ that you give to your brothers and sisters. In you, as in the bread and wine of the Eucharist, God the Father starts with the *human* and brings out the *beyond-the-human*. God the Father gives you a share in a ministry that humans could not deserve and would not dare to ask for on their own. Your call to serve is as unexpected and as undeserved as the young boy's at the multiplication of the loaves and fishes (John 6:1-15). When Jesus wanted to feed the large, hungry crowd of his hearers, he didn't ask the Father to create loaves and fishes out of thin air. He could have, but he didn't. Jesus began this great miracle with loaves and fishes provided by a young boy. How happy and surprised that boy must have felt in knowing that Jesus had chosen to use his loaves and fishes in so great a miracle! The boy and the crowd that shared his lunch realized that God likes to start with the human when acting for and with human beings. God starts with the *human*—with *us*—to lead us beyond human possibilities. That is what Jesus did for the hungry crowd on the hillside in Galilee; that is what Jesus does for those of us who accept God's call to ministry and for those we serve.

Through your humble service as a minister of Communion, God unites you to your fellow members of the Body of Christ and actually forms all of you into that Body. But God doesn't do this without the *human*; God loves the human too much to ignore it. An extraordinary minister's human, personal, in-terior qualities will either build up or tear down the Body of Christ, that temple for God in the Spirit made up of brothers and sisters in Christ. The "Order for the Commissioning of Extraordinary Ministers of Holy Communion" contains words that are worth recalling often: "In this ministry, you must be examples of Christian living in faith and conduct; you must strive to grow in holiness through this sacrament of unity and love. Remember that, though many, we are one body because we share the one bread and one cup."[9]

There must be an essential unity between your life inside and outside the liturgy, as the liturgical scholar Aidan Kavanagh states: "The common end for which the diverse liturgical ministries work is not a ceremony but a corporate life in faithful communion with all God's holy people and holy things. For this reason liturgical ministers should never be seen to do in the liturgy what they are not regularly seen to do outside the liturgy."[10]

To put this another way: your service as ministers inside the liturgy should only make visible the faith and love you are seen to manifest outside the liturgy. Generous self-giving, conformed to the pattern of Christ's self-giving unto death, must mark both your interior and exterior life, both inside and outside the liturgy. St. Augustine exhorted his hearers to such self-giving while praising St. Lawrence, deacon and martyr, who had ministered the chalice of the Lord's Blood: "Just as he had partaken of a gift of self at the table of the Lord, so he prepared to offer such a gift. In his life he loved Christ; in his death he followed in his footsteps."[11] Similarly, your love for Christ present in the Eucharist and in his people will make the bread and wine you minister to others genuine signs of Christ's self-sacrifice and *your own*. The bread and wine that you minister to others will be outward signs of the love that flows from the heart of Christ and from your own heart.

"If, then, you want to understand the body of Christ," says St. Augustine, "remember what the Apostle says: 'You are the body of Christ and members thereof' (1 Cor 12:27). If, then, you are the body of Christ and his members, it is your mystery which is set forth on the Lord's table; it is your own mystery that you receive. . . . You say 'Amen' to what you are, and in saying 'Amen' you subscribe to it. For you hear the words 'The body of Christ,' and you answer 'Amen.' Be members of the body of Christ, then, so that your 'Amen' might be authentic."[12] As extraordinary ministers of Holy Communion, you join with your brothers and sisters to say "Amen" to Christ as you receive him in the Eucharist; you also lead your brothers and sisters, through their "Amen," to make a personal act of faith in the Christ who is present in the Eucharist and in themselves. Let your "Amen" to being a member of the Body of Christ be true, so that you can help make others' "Amen" to being members of the Body of Christ also be true. The bishops of the United States call for this true "Amen" in their statement *Christian Commitment*: the liturgical ministries, "As special ways of living out the baptismal life of faith . . . demand a renewal of faith in view of the new charge given by the community to the individual. These moments of personal dedication demand reflection, prayer, and discernment so that the decisions to be made may be truly responsive to God's call."[13]

Such reflection, prayer, and discernment are not one-time-only nourishment, but a necessary diet for sustaining a life of generous service to God's people, both inside and outside the liturgy. Your life as an extraordinary minister of Holy Communion must be one of both *being* and *giving* the Body of Christ. Let your "Amen" to that life of service be real and complete. Then you will find great joy in the Lord who chooses to be present in you, in those you serve, and in the Eucharist that forms you into his Body.

Being and Giving
the Body of Christ
Practical Suggestions

And whatever you do, in word or in deed, do everything in the name of the Lord Jesus. . . . (Col 3:17a)

The following suggestions are directed to extraordinary ministers of Holy Communion generally. Of course, there is no such thing as a "generic" minister of Communion, because each minister is a unique person commissioned for service to a particular community, and particular aspects of ministry in that community (for example, the arrangement of the worship space) will influence each minister's service. Thus there is no attempt to answer the question of whether ministers of Communion should occupy special places in the sanctuary during the entire eucharistic celebration, or the question of whether they should wear distinctive signs of ministry (badges, crosses, or vestments). Such signs may be valuable if they truly help ministers of Holy Communion to serve others better. For example, crosses worn by ministers should remind them and those they serve of Christ's sacrifice on the cross, his self-offering that we are to make our own in the Eucharist; crosses or badges should not be sacred jewelry worn for show.

In some places, the giving of "Communion blessings" to young children and other noncommunicants is customary. These blessings by the minister fulfill a psychological need for noncommunicants to "receive something" when others receive

Communion. These blessings may take the form of a small sign of the cross on the forehead, a larger one over the person, or a hand laid on the person's head, with or without words. An extraordinary minister can give such a blessing just as clergy do. But this practice is not required, and it is extraneous to the purpose of the Communion procession: coming forward to receive the Body and Blood of Christ. Also, such blessings are redundant since everyone in the assembly shares in the priest's blessing at the end of Mass.

The *General Instruction of the Roman Missal,* which gives official directives for the celebration of the Eucharist, has very few words about the proper dress of ministers of Communion: "lay ministers may wear the alb or other suitable vesture or other appropriate and dignified clothing."[14] The "Rite of Distributing Holy Communion by a Special Minister" prescribes "the vestments customary in the country, or clothing in keeping with this sacred ministry."[15] Certainly attire as casual as shorts and T-shirts is unacceptable dress for servants at the eucharistic table. The questions of proper seating, proper dress, and distinctive signs of ministry, and the washing of hands before and after giving Communion should be answered by the group of ministers themselves in consultation with the liturgy committee and the pastor; they should not be answered by decree of the pastor.

There are only a few suggestions for the ministry of Communion to the sick because the particular persons who are served (the mildly and seriously ill, the elderly, the homebound, prisoners, the dying of all ages) and the particular setting where this ministry takes place (a specific room or hospital or nursing home) will shape each minister's service. The tasks of those who minister within the liturgical celebration differ from the tasks of those who carry the Eucharist to the sick. Those who minister to the sick need special preparation (listening skills, education in the aging process, and study of the theology of sickness and death) that differs from that needed by ministers within the liturgical assembly. The liturgy committee should provide opportunities for the necessary instruction and training for both kinds of eucharistic ministry, as well as periodic "days of reflection and renewal" for liturgical ministers.

Ministry of Communion within the Assembly

1. You have a unique and special function to perform at each liturgy: the ministry of Communion. Thus you should not "double up" by serving as lector, usher, or song leader at one and the same liturgy. Such a practice can appear unintentionally as an attempt on your part to monopolize the liturgy, whereas the cooperation of a variety of liturgical ministers and the assembly they serve should highlight the communal ownership of the liturgy. It is understandable that an emergency might require you to serve in more than one ministry, but because of the need for respecting the variety and integrity of all ministries, such a practice should never be planned. The liturgy committee periodically should insure that there are sufficient ministers of Holy Communion to avoid the placing of unnecessary or undesirable burdens on them. The Bishops' Committee on the Liturgy *Newsletter* correctly states:

> As a general principle it is by far preferable to increase the number of eucharistic ministers than to have a minister function at several Masses on any particular day. The extraordinary minister should fulfill his/her role at the Mass in which he/she participates and

should not simply be assigned and waiting (in the sacristy, rectory or some other place) to distribute communion at several celebrations. Certainly in any given parish a sufficient number of qualified persons can be found to function as extraordinary ministers at the Sunday Masses which they attend and thus render it unnecessary for any extraordinary ministers to assist at more than one Mass. Here is a case where a too strict limitation of the number of special ministers would frustrate the proper development of this liturgical ministry.[16]

2. The sharing of the Body and Blood of Christ brings us into communion with him and with each other. This communion with other persons requires you to make the sharing of the Eucharist as personal as possible. You must, above all else, be truly present to others in the brief moment you share with them in the act of Communion. Yours is not the cold efficiency of vending machines, but the warming love owed to your brothers and sisters in Christ, fellow members of the very Body of Christ that you are sharing with them. Your ministry of Communion will be satisfying to you, as well as to those you serve, to the degree that you are as personal and person-centered as Jesus was.

3. Try to be caring about and at ease with the people you serve, both inside and outside the liturgy. Such care and ease are difficult to manifest during the liturgy if they are not part of a person's whole life. Avoid the obstacles that come with undue regard for a person's status in the community or for distinctions of class, sex, age, or race. All who gather at the table of the Lord are brothers and sisters in the Lord; their assembly is marked by equality in Jesus Christ. In this climate of equality (the only climate in which the Lord Jesus makes himself present), those who serve others must be inviting to all God's people. They must give every member of the assembly the gracious welcome that God the Father extends to the honored guests at the wedding banquet of God's Son. This welcome is enfleshed in the liturgical ministers who serve their brothers and sisters in the assembly, that family of hungry children who desire to be filled with God's life like the Communion cups themselves:

Silver chalices
gold-plated chalices
ceramic chalices
waiting in rows
to receive their precious contents:
each different in brilliance
in shape
in color
yet each receives in full measure
the blood beyond all price,
the refreshing drink of salvation.
Each Christian
waiting with others
to receive the precious gift:
each different in brilliance
in shape
in color
receives in full measure
the blood beyond all price,
the refreshing drink of salvation:
Christ's blood, given for all.[17]

One group that deserves particularly reverent service is the disabled. We might easily decide that it would be an act of hospitality to bring Communion to them in their places in church, and thus spare them the possible difficulty of coming forward to a Communion station. Some disabled persons who are physically unable to come forward genuinely might appreciate such thoughtful hospitality. Yet for others, such a practice would be a silent act of *in*hospitality: the disabled may have a genuine psychological and spiritual need to join their brothers and sisters in coming forward to receive their Lord in Holy Communion and thus celebrate their equality as members of the Body of Christ. Eucharistic ministers should not decide for the disabled how they are to receive their Lord, but should ask the disabled courteously how they might best serve them in the ministry of Communion.

4. *Haste* in sharing the Body and Blood of Christ is perhaps the habit most destructive to your ministry. The bishops of the United States have declared: "It is of the greatest importance that the minister avoid all rush and haste. [The] ministration of

Communion should be done with dignity and reverence."[18] Dignity and reverence are the antidote to the poison of haste.

If we are concerned that people receive Communion reverently (and we should be), then we must be just as concerned that we are not racing to complete the sharing of Communion as quickly as possible. My mother was correct when she stated that the giving of Communion is not like piecework! You will avoid the temptation to rush if you are dignified and reverent, relaxed yourself and making others relaxed, careful but not fussy. The sharing of Communion is a God-given opportunity to embody the desirable qualities expressed in an advertisement for China Airlines: "Civility, Ceremony, Respect: The Sign of Service." The sharing of Communion is a divine/human ceremony that requires civility and respect; these qualities must be a sign of your service.

5. The ministry of Communion is only for those who can look another person in the eye with comfort and touch another person with ease. The human action of sharing the Body and Blood of Christ requires ocular, verbal, and tactile contact to express personal communion. The person to whom you are ministering deserves your full attention. Your meeting with the communicant is only for a brief moment; you can't rehearse it with the person before it happens or stage it again later. The Lord's eucharistic gifts are infinite and can't be diminished or lost through his minister's weakness or mistakes. Yet the people you serve can receive only what they are prepared to receive—and your attitude and actions are part of their immediate preparation for Communion. If you are gazing down the approaching line of people or scanning the congregation instead of giving full attention to the person before you, most of the encounter's *human* value will be lost. The Lord Jesus will still be present, but you, his servant, will have obscured his presence to a greater or lesser extent. If you are able to disregard everything and everyone else in the moment of Communion, you will be able to welcome the person before you with undivided attention and unmistakable reverence. Such is the welcome that Jesus gave to notorious sinners and near-saints, to the just and the unjust, to joyful children and sorrowful adults;

such is the welcome you can give to your sisters and brothers as you serve them in Jesus' name.

When a communicant approaches you, there is fulfilled that saying of Jesus: "Where two or three are gathered together in my name, there am I in the midst of them" (Matt 18:20). When and where could this saying be more completely fulfilled? Christ is present in his Body and Blood; he is present also in the communicant and in the minister who come together in his name: "The Body of Christ." "Amen!" "The Blood of Christ." "Amen!"

You profess your own faith in saying "The Body of Christ" and "The Blood of Christ" as you serve your brothers and sisters. You also call forth the faith of those you serve as they respond, "Amen!" It can happen (and hopefully will) that their response of faith will strengthen your ability to call forth that response. It was my privilege to celebrate Mass weekly as a member of the chaplaincy team at St. Benedict's Monastery, the sister community of St. John's Abbey. There it was my special privilege to give Communion to Sister Eva, one of the oldest sisters in the community. When she approached me to receive Communion, there was absolutely no doubt in her mind (nor in mine!) about what she was doing: she was receiving her Lord! Everything about her posture and bearing—her serene face, her carefully outstretched hands, her reverent nod to her eucharistic Lord (and also to me, unworthy minister though I was), her momentary smile as she held the host in her hands—everything told me that she had entered into this holy moment totally. And I wondered: have *I* entered into this holy moment as completely as she has? Her reverence in receiving Communion from my hands deepened my own reverence in giving Communion to her and to all who followed her. As I gave the strengthening food of the Eucharist to Sister Eva, she gave strength to me: a wonderful exchange!

Everyone who receives Communion from your hands has a right to the full human and divine value of this holy moment. Yet at times you may feel that your psychological and physical state makes you more of a hindrance than a help. At such times, try to perform your ministry with faith, prayerfulness, and care, regardless of your current mood or feeling. The spirit of joy and peace within you—even if hiding deep down inside of you—will shine through despite what your emotions tell you at the moment. The Lord Jesus gives his servants a special gift of strength as they begin to serve his sacred meal to his (and their) brothers and sisters. As you wait to begin your service during the liturgy, look out over the congregation and say to yourself: "This assembly—this gathering of God's holy people of which I am a part—is the Body of Christ made visible, audible, and tangible here and now, in this place, at this time. I have accepted God's call to help this assembly, the Body of Christ, to be united with Christ their Head in Holy Communion. Everything I do and say should help them to receive the Lord Jesus more reverently and lovingly. With your help, Lord Jesus, I will serve them well." Only by joyfully and prayerfully inviting others to the feast—even when it is difficult to do so—can you enjoy the feast yourself.

Sharing the Bread

6. After each communicant has stopped in front of you, *speak to that person*; don't address the air or the bread or the cup, because you are eliciting an "Amen!" from a person. Raise the bread slightly and look the person in the eye in a friendly manner, and say as if you mean it "The Body of Christ." Speak loudly enough so that hard-of-hearing persons will be able to say their "Amen!" at the proper time. Wait for the communicant to bow his/her head before the sacrament in the prescribed gesture of reverence and say "Amen." Placing the bread on the tongue or in the hand before a communicant can say "Amen!" indicates a lack of attentiveness in the minister. Pressing down slightly on the bread as you place it on the tongue or in the hand (and touching the hand) will help the communicant know that you have really placed it there; this is an extra act of hospitality for those persons who have difficulty in determining this.

7. There are three kinds of necessary contact in the sharing of Communion: ocular, verbal, and tactile. Dare to let your eyes meet those of the communicant and reflect the wonder of God's love in the Eucharist. Dare to let your voice announce God's in-

vitation to the banquet of eternal life. Dare to let your hands touch those of the communicant as they minister God's holy gifts. Dare to let the communicant feel the texture of the bread and of *your own hand*; dare to feel the communicant's hand (it may be as rough or smooth as your own). It would be possible to place the bread in a person's hand in a more "antiseptic" way, but at the loss of so much of the human, personal warmth of this moment.

There is something especially beautiful about helping people to receive Communion in the hand. Romano Guardini has written that "the soul's chief instruments and clearest mirrors are the face and hands."[19] Even hands that are permanently soiled (like a mechanic's) are beautiful: they testify that a person's livelihood can be seen in the hands, hands that receive the Lord's saving touch and our reverent one.

Sad to say, not everyone has learned the proper way to receive Communion in the hand. If you observe large numbers of children or adults coming forward for Communion without giving a clear indication of their desire to receive in the hand, or snatching the bread with their fingers, or failing to bow their head and respond "Amen!" at the proper time, you should suggest to your pastor and the liturgy committee that instruction is needed. Such a suggestion and the subsequent instruction from the priest or in the parish bulletin will help you to be a better minister of Holy Communion.

8. Allow communicants to indicate the manner in which they wish to receive. Small children sometimes hold their extended hands rather low, and the plate you are holding may make it difficult for you to see their upturned palms; you may have to adjust the plate accordingly. Place the bread in the person's outstretched hands or on the tongue reverently. This is not an action like handing change over the counter at the corner store, but like handing over a treasured family heirloom (for example, a diamond ring that you inherited from your great-grandmother). How careful you would be while handling such a treasure! Can we be less careful with ministering the Body and Blood of Christ?

Sharing the Cup

9. There should be two cup ministers for each bread minister because the sharing of the cup usually takes more time than the sharing of the bread. If you are serving as a cup minister, stand a fair distance (five or six feet) away from the bread minister; this will allow freedom of movement for the communicants and keep the Communion procession moving. Present the cup with a careful but inviting gesture, and say: "The Blood of Christ," again waiting for the communicant to bow his/her head before the sacrament and say "Amen."

10. As you hand the cup to the communicant, allow your hands to touch naturally. Let the communicant take the cup with both hands, but you might help guide the cup to the lips of small children. After the communicant drinks and returns the cup to you, wipe the rim (outside and inside) with the purificator (napkin) and turn the cup a quarter turn before repeating the procedure for the next communicant. Perhaps directions for receiving from the cup should be announced before certain eucharistic celebrations (for example, Christmas Midnight Mass) for the benefit of those who may not be familiar with this practice.

11. Your actions as you minister the bread and cup are very simple ones. Yet as you do them, you should remember that you are doing them in memory of Jesus Christ. Through your gracious words and gestures, you are repeating his invitation to his disciples: "Take, eat . . . this is my Body. Take, drink . . . this is my Blood. Receive my Body and Blood, given for you." Christ's self-giving *and your own* must be enfleshed in your ministering of the Body and Blood of Christ if his invitation is to appear genuine. You must imitate Christ in his self-giving, for he remains the most perfect giver of self that the world will ever know.

12. Try to make your giving of the bread and cup to others as graceful and reverent as possible. Your reverence for the Eucharist and for those you serve will be happily contagious.

Walk with reverence as you approach the sanctuary. The *Norms for the Distribution and Reception of Holy Communion Under Both Kinds in the Dioceses of the United States*, approved by the United

States bishops in 2001 and confirmed by the Vatican in 2002, state: "If extraordinary ministers of Holy Communion are required by pastoral need, they approach the altar as the priest receives Communion" (no. 38), so that they themselves will be ready to receive Communion. But extraordinary ministers can enter the sanctuary during the "Lamb of God" and wait reverently to the side or rear of the altar. Only a deacon or concelebrating priests may assist the priest in breaking the bread and placing it in other vessels (*Norms*, no. 37).

"After the priest has concluded his own Communion, he distributes Communion to the extraordinary ministers, assisted by the deacon" (*Norms*, no. 38). It is fitting that the priest or deacon minister the bread and cup to you; cafeteria-style self-service is not appropriate for those who symbolize humble service to others. Then the priest or deacon hands the sacred vessels to the extraordinary ministers for ministering Communion to the assembly (*Norms*, no. 38). And to make this absolutely clear, the *Norms* tell us that "the practice of extraordinary ministers of Holy Communion waiting to receive Holy Communion until after the distribution of Holy Communion is not in accord with liturgical law" (no. 39).

Why this insistence that extraordinary ministers receive Communion before sharing the Body and Blood of Christ with the assembly? This order helps us to grasp a basic truth of the Eucharist we celebrate: Jesus Christ is the sole giver of this sacred food, the only host at this sacred banquet. Everyone else is a guest, including the priest, deacon, and extraordinary ministers of Holy Communion. Christ is the giver and the gift; we are all receivers. Reverently and humbly receiving the Body and Blood of Christ from the priest or deacon may be the best immediate preparation that extraordinary ministers can have for reverently and humbly ministering the Eucharist to others. This sacrament is the fullest sign of Christ's self sacrifice unto death. In receiving it before the assembly does, extraordinary ministers are invited to make some of Christ's self-giving their own in the words and gestures of their sacred ministry.

Where the Communion of a large number of ministers may become lengthy, "the presider could minister to the deacon and/or to two communion ministers. Then they in turn could minister to the others so that the communion of the assembly may begin without delay."[20]

Stand with reverence as you receive a plate or cup from the priest or deacon and take your position at a Communion station. Standing with your feet about six to eight inches apart will give comfort and balance at the same time. Your posture should indicate that you are relaxed but ready for attentive service. Your demeanor should be that of a caring host or hostess, not that of a soldier presenting the colors at graveside.

Hold the plate and cup with reverence. Hold them as if they and especially their contents were very precious, but not in a fussy manner that calls too much attention to itself and results in accidents. Gabe Huck rightly notes that a strong reverence for what you carry "is to be seen and felt by all: not a false humility, but a strong sense of joy and delight in the very sharing of the Lord's body and blood. That can translate to how the plate is picked up and carried, how the minister stands, how the cup or plate is later returned to a side table. It may be as simple a matter as using both hands, rather than one, to carry the cup or plate."[21] Resist the temptation to slide plates and cups across slippery altar cloths even when you need to move them only a few inches, or to grab cups by the rim: God gave the cup a stem for a purpose.

If you need to break some pieces of bread into smaller ones lest communicants be deprived of the Eucharist, ask a communicant to hold the plate for you; this minimizes the possibility of parts of hosts flying onto the floor as you break them. If your congregation regularly shares a more substantial eucharistic bread, a person to hold the plate might be a welcome helper. Where a large number of communicants can result in rapid emptying of Communion vessels, a Communion minister could be ready to bring extra bread and wine to the Communion stations, as well as to help collect unused bread and wine and vessels.

If you or a communicant should drop a piece of bread (and this can happen despite all cautions taken), gracefully stoop down and pick it up (often a communicant is too startled to do so). Keep this bread apart so that you can dispose of it reverently after Communion or after Mass. There may be a small, covered bowl of water near the tabernacle where you can let this piece of bread dissolve; later you can pour the water into a special sink in the sacristy called a *sacrarium*. Or you could simply consume this bread in an inconspicuous manner (the danger from germs is minimal). If the wine should spill, someone should wash the area immediately using a clean cloth and a vessel of water. The water should be poured into the *sacrarium*; the cloth should be placed with the soiled altar linen.

Remove the unused bread and wine with reverence. "Even after Communion the Lord remains present under the species. Accordingly, when Communion has been distributed, the sacred particles remaining are to be consumed or taken by the competent minister to the place where the Eucharist is reserved."[22] Super-scrupulosity is not to be cultivated, but reasonable effort must be made to avoid carelessly giving scandal or unwittingly appearing to deny Roman Catholic belief about Christ's presence in the Eucharist. Crumbs should be disposed of reverently after each Mass, either by consuming them or by mixing them with water and drinking the mixture or pouring it into the *sacrarium*. Communion cups containing wine should not be left to vie with collection baskets for space on sacristy counters; the extra wine should not be reserved in the tabernacle (unless it is needed for Communion to the sick), but should be consumed reverently by the ministers after Communion or after Mass.

Your reverence will be evident in all your actions: in the way you walk about the sanctuary, hold your hands, genuflect, place the bread and hand over the cup, return plates and cups to side tables, remove the unused bread and wine. Your movements should be careful and deliberate, although natural and honest. You must serve with dignity and humility, and thus enflesh reverence for the whole Body of Christ, Head and members.

13. Routine is the death of reverence. You will know that you are succumbing to routine when your voice becomes sing-songy, or when you fail to wait for communicants to respond "Amen!," or when you angrily wonder why the whole congregation apparently decided to get into *your* line, or when you scan the approaching communicants and see only numbers and

not persons. Imagine Jesus looking down the row of apostles at the Last Supper and counting how many more sets of feet he had to wash. Unthinkable!

When you find yourself becoming routine or checking how long the lines are, it is time to refocus on the significance of the actions you are performing. Mentally stop and imagine that you are giving Communion to one person only: the next person coming up to you! Imagine how careful and reverent you would be if you were to give Communion to only one person at each liturgy. Yet, in a sense, that is what you are doing. No matter whether you give Communion to ten people or ten times that many, each person receives Communion from your hands *once*. Your presence and actions will have much to do with how that person receives the Lord in Holy Communion that day, for good or ill. Such is the challenge and responsibility of your call to ministry.

Former Bishop Kenneth Untener of Saginaw, Michigan, attested that your service "takes a lot of skill. It takes concentration. It takes verbal and nonverbal expressiveness. It takes practice. And it takes much love. I am not saying that it should be dramatic or over-done. It should simply be real and expressive. The person who truly *ministers* the Eucharist to a hundred people should be tired at the end. It takes a lot out of one."[23] The strain on the vocal cords and back muscles is part of the light burden of the Lord Jesus, who strengthens us for and in our ministry.

14. As you complete your service within the liturgy and return to your place, the eucharistic celebration will soon be over. You may carry Communion to the sick after Mass; but as you complete your service to the assembly of God's people, recall the words of a hymn called "Reflection Song":

> Too soon we rise; we go our separate ways:
> The feast, Tho' not the love, is past and gone;
> The bread and wine consumed: yet all our days
> You are still with us—our shield and sun.

Those who have truly received Christ's service in the Eucharist, the service Christ gives them at your hands, will know that they must serve their brothers and sisters in return. The liturgy "is in itself a stream flowing from God's great goodness; it does not merely teach, it leads to love."[24] Your gracious lesson and example as a minister of Holy Communion will lead others to generous service of their neighbors.

Ministry of Communion to the Sick and Homebound

Laypersons who bring the Eucharist to the sick and those confined to their homes—possibly to members of their own families—are reviving a practice that appears to have flourished widely from the second to the early fifth centuries. In these early centuries of Christianity, laypersons carried the eucharistic bread home with them from the Sunday Eucharist and kept it in their homes; there, the Body of Christ became the family's "daily bread" as they reverently consumed the Eucharist together before their regular meal.

Around the year 150, St. Justin Martyr noted that in Rome, deacons took Communion to those Christians who were absent from the assembly because of illness or imprisonment for their faith. Perhaps he included this detail in his defense of Christianity in order to give his pagan readers some accurate information about it. The inclusion of the absent Christians in the assembly's worship through the eucharistic food sent to them struck the pagans as a very strange and distinctive element of Christian worship. Pagans believed that they had to be physically present at the temple if they were to benefit from their worship. But this was not true for Christians then, and it is not true for Christians now.

1. The Christian worshiping assembly embraces those who are unable to be present in the person of those whom it commissions to carry Communion to their sisters and brothers. "And so it is most fitting that they go directly from the assembly's Sunday Eucharist; sending them forth to do their ministry could be incorporated into the dismissal rite of the mass."[25] The ministers could gather in the sanctuary or in the main aisle before the altar to receive a special blessing, after which they could lead the other ministers down the aisle during the recessional music. In

this way, the assembly of Sunday worshipers would be visibly linked to the sick and aged who are unable to participate fully at the Sunday Eucharist.

2. According to the document Holy Communion and Worship of the Eucharist Outside Mass, "The eucharist for communion outside a church is to be carried in a pyx or other covered vessel; the vesture of the minister and the manner of carrying the eucharist should be appropriate and in accord with local circumstances."[26] Formerly, the priest or acolyte carrying Communion to the sick at home or in the hospital maintained absolute silence. Today, Communion ministers might find themselves in situations where the breaking of strict silence would not equal irreverence (for example, returning a neighbor's greeting on the street). A certain seriousness as you carry the Eucharist can prepare you to serve your sick brothers and sisters prayerfully and can prevent the casualness which is inappropriate to such a ritual.

3. Your familiarity with the rite of "Communion in Ordinary Circumstances" should be apparent all the way from the greeting you give to the sick person to your farewell. Yet familiarity with the official rite should not mean slavish adherence to the rite. Particular circumstances of the sick person's environment, or physical or psychological condition, may make the celebration less tidy than it appears in the rite (and you should not blame the sick person or yourself for this). For example, some words of pleasant conversation between you and the sick person might be expected to follow the conclusion of the rite of Communion (after allowing the communicant some time for silent prayer and thanksgiving). Yet there might be occasions when such conversation could better *precede* the rite of Communion (as when the sick person just can't wait to tell you some good news!). The official rite does begin rather formally, and a more familiar form of greeting and introduction could be the prelude to the sick person's more fruitful reception of the Eucharist. You, the minister, must know both the rite and the people you serve well enough so that you can easily adapt the very general rite for the benefit of very specific persons. Common sense is as desirable for liturgical ministers as for anyone else; in fact, it is a necessity, not a luxury.

4. The sick to whom you minister may ask about the Church's regulations on the eucharistic fast, and they will appreciate your accurate explanation of the present legislation to them. This legislation is contained in the revised Code of Canon Law, promulgated by Pope John Paul II on January 25, 1983. The first and third paragraphs of Canon 919 declare that

> One who is to receive the Most Holy Eucharist is to abstain from any food or drink, with the exception only of water and medicine, for at least the period of one hour before Holy Communion.
>
> Those who are advanced in age or who suffer from any infirmity, as well as those who take care of them, can receive the Most Holy Eucharist even if they have taken something during the previous hour.[27]

Thus, if elderly or ill persons (and those who care for them) have taken food, drink, or medicine only a short while before your visit, they are not prevented from receiving Communion.

Although it may be preferable to bring Communion directly from the Sunday Eucharist, it is good to ask sick persons about the best time for your visit and arrange your schedule accordingly. Sick persons' rhythms of rest, meals, and medication may suggest a later morning hour or some more convenient time; you and your fellow ministers of Communion can arrange for earlier and later visits in the various areas of the parish.

Insofar as they can conveniently do so, those who are with the sick should prepare the following before you bring Communion:

1) a table covered with a linen cloth upon which the Eucharist will be placed
2) lighted candles
3) where it is customary, a vessel of holy water and a sprinkler or a small branch.

5. The Second Vatican Council insisted that sacred celebrations should include a "more ample, more varied, and more suitable reading from sacred scripture."[28] All the revised sacramental rites now include a Liturgy of the Word to help express the meaning of the sacramental action. The rite of Communion

of the sick includes a large number of Scripture readings, one of which you or someone present should choose (in advance) and proclaim; the sick person might indicate which reading is the most appropriate at a particular time. Remember to speak loudly and slowly when ministering to the hard-of-hearing. You might choose to read one of the Scripture readings of the Sunday or feast-day Eucharist; then you might briefly explain the reading in the light of the sick person's needs, or you might briefly summarize the homily that you heard at the Eucharist that day. Thus you will share both the Word and the sacrament that have nourished your parish community, the nourishment to which the sick members of the community also have a right. Before your visit, you might prepare some general intercessions (prayer of the faithful); you should invite those assembled to pray, and later you will say the concluding prayer, but it is desirable that someone else announce the intentions. Your parish might provide you with a copy of the general intercessions used at the Sunday Eucharist, which you could adapt for use with the sick.

6. Why not invite others in the community (and especially the members of your own family) to accompany you as you carry Communion to the sick? Both the sick and those who accompany you will come to a greater awareness of their identity as "one body in Christ and individually members one of another" (Rom 12:5). The sick are not *objects* of ministry, but full participants in a ministering community which embraces them as the suffering members of its own body, the Body of Christ. This embrace can become tangible in a prayerful laying-on of hands by you and by all who have gathered, a soothing and healing gesture that could be a regular part of your ministry.

7. The parish bulletin or newsletter contains important information that is of interest to the sick (for example, announcements of communal anointings, lists of the hospitalized, death notices), and your bringing a copy to them will help them feel more a part of the community's activities, even if they cannot share fully in them. Some parishes also provide audio tapes of the Sunday homily.

8. The occasion of your carrying Communion to a sick person ideally should be one important moment in that person's rhythm of personal and communal prayer. Thus you should be prepared to suggest resources for prayer to help the sick person pray more regularly and fervently; you will be able to do this more easily if you value and practice personal and communal prayer yourself.

Lay-Led
Communion Services

More and more we have seen the Communion service, led by a layperson, substituted for the Mass in parishes without priests. Is the Communion service a poor substitute for the Mass? No, in the sense that both of these official liturgies of the Church celebrate Christ's saving death and resurrection and enable us to share in them by receiving his Body and Blood. But the worldwide phenomenon of parishes without priests to serve them and preside at the Sunday Eucharist raises some serious questions about the Communion service as a regular form of parish worship.

In the traditional observance of Sunday in the Church, there ideally come together three key elements: time, community, and event. In other words, on the Lord's *day*, the Lord's *people* celebrate the Lord's *Supper*. Where this ideal form of Sunday worship becomes impossible, the ministry of lay leaders is becoming customary. This practice has been a controversial one, however. Many have raised questions such as: If the Communion service becomes the usual Sunday or weekday worship in priestless parishes, will not the people's experience of giving thanks over bread and cup be diminished or lost? Will not the Eucharist increasingly be seen as a thing given to them, not an action done by them?

The complete eucharistic celebration on Sunday is a full expression of the priestly calling of the entire people of God and is a centuries-old Roman Catholic tradition. To what extent are we prepared to depart from it in favor of lay-led Communion services on Sunday? This is a debate that will continue for some time in the Church. In the meantime, many extraordinary eucharistic ministers will be called upon to lead such services in their parish community.

Practical Suggestions

The basic rite according to which you lead Communion services is contained in the 1973 document *Holy Communion and Worship of the Eucharist outside Mass* (henceforth referred to as *Holy Communion*). But you will also want to be familiar with the *Directory for Sunday Celebrations in the Absence of a Priest* (henceforth referred to as *Directory*) if you lead such celebrations, and with the revised rite for the United States based on the *Directory's* provisions.

The presentation of the gifts and the Eucharistic Prayer are not included in a Communion service, but nothing prescribed or beneficial should be lacking in this rite (for example, a full Liturgy of the Word and music, if possible) or in your leadership (for example, revealing God's graciousness to the worshipers

through your words and gestures). Good leaders of worship are like clear glass vessels that do not obscure, but rather reveal the contents of the liturgy. A fine crystal goblet enhances the appearance of the wine inside it, but the cartoon characters on a glass call attention to themselves. Leading a Communion service means doing everything one can to help a holy people to receive the holy gift of Eucharist.

Your vesture should be what is appropriate to the role of leading and what has been approved by the bishop. The alb is the basic liturgical vesture for ministers of both sexes.

A lay leader does not use the presidential chair (*Directory*, no. 40), but should lead from a place where he or she can be seen and heard by the assembly. The roles of reader, cantor, etc., are to be shared among suitable persons (*Directory*, no. 40).

Introductory Rites

The *Directory* does not indicate the content of these rites, while *Holy Communion* (nos. 27–28) generally follows the Order of Mass.

An opening hymn or gathering music, as well as an entrance procession, are not prescribed in either document, but singing at the beginning of the service can help unify the assembly. The sign of the cross, also not prescribed, would seem to be fitting at this time. "The layperson is not to use words that are proper to a priest or deacon and is to omit rites that are too readily associated with the Mass, for example, greetings—especially 'The Lord be with you'—and dismissals, since these might give the impression that the layperson is a sacred minister" (*Directory*, no. 39). See *Holy Communion*, no. 27, for a suggested form of greeting, but you may prepare your own. You might think of "greeting" as being equivalent to brief introductory words that help the assembled worshipers focus their hearts and minds on this *particular* celebration: sharing the Body and Blood of Christ on this feast or occasion.

Next follows the penitential rite (*Holy Communion*, no. 28), for which the Sacramentary includes three forms. The third form (C) is not intended to be a public confession of faults, verbalized soul-searching, or a communal examination of conscience. Rather, it is a series of invocations by which the assembly confesses (actually *professes*) their trust in Christ's power to save them from sin. One of the Sacramentary's eight examples of form C may be used, or other invocations may be composed for a particular feast, season, or occasion. They should be addressed to Christ the Lord, theologically correct and well-phrased.

An opening prayer is not prescribed for ordinary celebrations, but the *Directory* states that on Sundays and solemnities the opening prayer and the prayer after Communion are taken from the Sacramentary (no. 36).

Celebration of the Word of God

One or more readings from Scripture follow the introductory rites. They are taken "either from the Mass of the day or from the votive Masses of the Holy Eucharist or the Precious Blood," which are found in the *Lectionary for Mass* (*Holy Communion*, no. 29). See *Holy Communion*, nos. 113–88, for an extensive list of possible and appropriate readings (for example, those for the votive Mass of the Sacred Heart). On Sundays and solemnities the readings assigned to the day in the Lectionary are used (*Directory*, no. 36).

After the first reading there is a psalm, song, or silent prayer. The acclamation before the gospel is not prescribed but is very appropriate. If it is used, it should be sung. The gospel is proclaimed without the customary greeting the priest uses, but only with: "A reading from the holy gospel according to . . . ."

Preaching is optional, but certainly welcome in order to better nourish the assembly from the two tables of Word and sacrament. The *Directory* permits a lay leader to give an "explanation of the readings," or there may be a period of silent reflection (no. 43). Or the pastor may prepare a homily and give it to the lay leader to read. Homilies by the Church Fathers (for example, those from the Office of Readings in the Liturgy of the Hours) and by other Catholic authors might serve well here. The profession of faith is normally recited on Sundays and solemnities.

The general intercessions conclude the celebration of the Word. The leader introduces them by addressing an opening invitation to prayer to the assembly (not by addressing a prayer to God). Someone else should announce the intentions at the lectern or another suitable place. This minister could stand next to the leader while announcing the intentions. This would serve to unify the prayer by providing a single focus.

You might be called upon to prepare the general intercessions as well as lead them. Some helpful resources are the sample intercessions at the back of the Sacramentary; Robert Hovda, "The Prayer of General Intercession," *Worship* 44 (October 1970); and Michael Kwatera, O.S.B., *Preparing the General Intercessions* (Collegeville: The Liturgical Press, 1996).

As a rule, the sequence of intentions is to be: (a) for the needs of the Church, (b) for public authorities and the salvation of the world, (c) for those oppressed by any need, (d) for the local community. A brief prayer by the leader concludes the general intercessions.

Thanksgiving

The *Directory* prescribes a "Thanksgiving" as part of the rite on Sundays, but this element would be fitting on other days as well. The thanksgiving takes one of the following forms: a) after the general intercessions or after the sharing of Communion, the leader invites the assembly to an act of thanksgiving, which may be: a psalm (for example, Psalms 100, 113, 118, 136, 147, or 150), a hymn or canticle (for example the *Glory to God* or Mary's *Magnificat*), or a litany sung or recited by all present. The leader and the assembly stand facing the altar for the thanksgiving; b) alternatively, before the Lord's Prayer that begins the Communion rite, the leader takes the Eucharist from the place of reservation, places it on the altar, and genuflects. Then, while kneeling before the sacrament, all sing or recite a hymn, psalm, or litany directed to Christ in the Eucharist. Your parish music ministers might be asked to suggest and lead suitable music.

The thanksgiving is not to take the form of a Eucharistic Prayer, nor are the prefaces and Eucharistic Prayers of the Sacramentary to be used (*Directory*, no. 45). This is to avoid confusing the Communion service with the full eucharistic celebration.

Communion Rite

The reserved Eucharist is taken from the tabernacle, placed on the altar, and honored with a genuflection.

The Lord's Prayer, introduced by the leader and sung or recited by all, now follows, unless the act of thanksgiving is to take place first (see *Directory*, no. 45). The words, "Deliver us, Lord, from every evil. . . ." are omitted. After the Lord's Prayer, the sign of peace is optional but welcome preparation for sharing Communion. Extend your hands widely, embracing the assembly, as you give the invitation, "Let us offer each other the sign of peace." Then share with those around you the ritual gesture that seals our unity in the peace of Christ.

After genuflecting, raise a piece of the consecrated bread over the plate and say, "This is the Lamb of God . . . ." (*Holy Communion*, no. 32). Wait for the assembly to respond, "Lord, I am not worthy . . . ." before receiving Communion.

The directions indicate that the leader and other ministers are to receive Communion before serving the assembly. During the sharing of Communion, a hymn may be sung.

When Communion is finished, the unused bread is gathered into containers at the altar or side table for placement in the tabernacle, the transfer to which might be done by another minister of Holy Communion. Crumbs should be disposed of reverently, either by consuming them or by mixing them with water and drinking the mixture, or by pouring it into the *sacrarium*. It is preferable that all Communion vessels be cleansed in the sacristy after the liturgy is over.

After the sharing of Communion, there may be a period of silence, or a psalm or song of praise may be sung (*Holy Communion*, no. 37). The *Directory* suggests various forms of thanksgiving at this point (no. 45). Any necessary announcements should be made before the concluding prayer, for which a number of options are provided (*Holy Communion*, nos. 38, 210–22). On Sundays and solemnities this prayer should be the one assigned to the day in the Sacramentary.

Concluding Rites

In concluding the Communion service, a lay leader invokes God's blessing on the assembly with one of the texts given in *Holy Communion* (no. 40), signing him/herself while doing so.

According to the *Directory* (no. 39), a lay leader is to omit the dismissal. But *Holy Communion* (no. 41) provides a dismissal ("Go in the peace of Christ") for use by the minister, presumably either ordained or lay.

An exit procession would be fitting only if there has been an entrance procession. As the procession forms, make the customary reverence to the altar (a low bow, or a genuflection if the tabernacle is behind the altar), and leave the sanctuary in the same order as at the beginning of the service. A final hymn or recessional music is not prescribed, but might help send the assembly forth to love and serve the Lord in the members of his Body.

The following outline lists the elements of the rite of giving Holy Communion outside Mass with the celebration of the Word. Parts in [ ] are fitting but not required according to the official rite.

Introductory Rites

— [Opening hymn or gathering music]
— Greeting
— Penitential Rite
— [Opening Prayer]

Celebration of the Word of God

— One or more readings from Scripture
— Psalm following first reading, or song or silent prayer
— [Gospel Acclamation before Gospel]
— [Homily]
— General Intercessions

Holy Communion

— Reserved Eucharist is brought to the altar, followed by genuflection
— Lord's Prayer
— Sign of peace may be exchanged
— Genuflection before "This is the Lamb of God . . . ."
— Giving of Communion, during which a hymn may be sung
— Eucharist is returned to the tabernacle
— Silence, or a psalm or song of praise may be sung
— Concluding Prayer, for which all stand (14 options)

Concluding Rite

— Blessing (simple, solemn, or prayer over the people)
— Dismissal
— [Final hymn or recessional music]

Looking for
the Perfect Eucharistic Minister

Its bouquet hinted of roses, its color was deep ruby, and its aftertaste was slightly sweet—the kind of wine that would enhance any altar. Such was the judgment of the clerical sippers at the Third International Seminar on Altar Wine, held May 16, 1992, at Cocconato d'Asti in northern Italy. Here the wine *Malvaxia Sincerum*, a local entry of Italy's Piedmont region, was deemed the best of a dozen products to grace the palates of the four elderly priest-judges.

This meeting aimed at promoting "ever more esteemed Mass wines," according to an organizer, Roberto Bava. The "religious tasting commission" rated the twelve competing wines from Spain, Italy, and California on a 0–20 point basis. *Malvaxia Sincerum*, the winning wine made from Italian malvasia grapes, was the fruit of a three-year research project aimed at finding "the perfect altar wine," Bava explained. In 1988, eight Italian clerics were asked to draw up characteristics of the ideal Mass wine. The profile that emerged was one of low alcoholic content (around 10 percent), not too sweet, and a deep red color—a move away from the white wine tradition in most Western churches.

So now you know what the perfect Mass wine is like. But what about the perfect *minister* of the consecrated wine, the ideal minister of the eucharistic bread? What are the characteristics of the ideal eucharistic minister?

First, the perfect eucharistic minister is *prayerful*. Eucharistic ministry is part of a larger whole of liturgical ministry: welcoming, leading, altar serving, proclaiming the Scriptures, preaching, leading song, singing in the choir, playing musical instruments. Every weekend, the perfect eucharistic minister prays for all who will serve as ministers to God's people on the Lord's day, both in the local community and elsewhere.

The perfect eucharistic minister *esteems teamwork*. When we assemble for worship, our roles and responsibilities vary, and rightly so. Thus, we expect to find a diversity of ministries within the liturgical assembly. What binds all these ministries together is *teamwork*. The cooperation of different yet complementary ministries must be found first in the hearts of those who minister, ordained and nonordained, before it can be seen to unify the liturgical celebration. The principle of teamwork that ought to shape our thinking and acting as liturgical ministers is love expressed in service: ". . . serve one another through love" (Gal 5:13).

The perfect eucharistic minister is *attentive* and *helpful*. No matter how well prepared we personally are for our ministry on any given day, no matter how well our liturgies are celebrated, things can go wrong (maybe you knew this already . . .).

Maybe, during the "Lamb of God," it becomes evident that the Communion cups haven't been placed in the sanctuary, or a scheduled minister hasn't showed up. It is precisely in such unexpected situations that the perfect eucharistic minister is *most* attentive and helpful, accomplishing whatever needs to be done, when it needs to be done, without waiting for a divine email to give permission or directions.

Also, the perfect eucharistic minister is willing and able to explain to visiting presiders how the Communion rite unfolds in the parish (for example, who ministers where). After Mass, the perfect eucharistic minister helps consume the remaining wine and cleans the vessels if expected to. Always, the perfect eucharistic minister does whatever needs to be done: carefully and effectively, minimizing confusion and embarrassment, not drawing attention to oneself and away from the important words and actions of the liturgy. All this makes the perfect eucharistic minister to be a "full service" servant, before, during, and after the liturgy.

The perfect eucharistic minister is *reverent*. We cannot ignore or underestimate the desirable impact that reverence has on others when we minister the Body and Blood of Christ. To do so is to ignore or underestimate how the "inner grace" of Christ becomes "outward sign" in and through us, the members of his Body in this world. How we speak our words and do our actions can express our reverence and so deepen it.

The perfect eucharistic minister is *unhasting*. "Haste is the death of devotion," declared St. Francis de Sales. The perfect eucharistic minister is not afraid to take a little extra time and care in ministering Communion to elderly and disabled persons, to small children, and to young parents with an infant in their arms or with several little ones in tow. Good liturgy requires a lot of patience on the part of a lot of people, and the perfect eucharistic minister will have lots of it.

The perfect eucharistic minister is *faithful to schedules*, as faithful as humanly possible. Emergencies can lead to unexpected absences, but the perfect eucharistic minister never assumes that someone else will cover a foreseen absence. Arranging a substitute when unable to minister is a mark of courtesy to the assembly and to the other eucharistic ministers.

The perfect eucharistic minister is *knowledgeable*: knowledgeable about this ministry and about the Eucharist. The commitment to serve as a eucharistic minister should be accompanied by some knowledge about the basis and guidelines for this ministry, and also some knowledge about the history, theology, and practice of the Eucharist. For example, those who bring Communion to the sick and homebound should be familiar with the present directives and rite for this ministry, since questions (for example, about the eucharistic fast) can be expected. Helpful information can be obtained through printed resources, audio-visual materials, the Internet, diocesan offices of worship, and liturgical conferences and workshops. The perfect eucharistic minister knows that this faith-filled ministry, like faith itself, must be constantly nourished by the Word of God, devotional reading, and other sources of spiritual formation and growth.

It's true that the perfect eucharistic minister may be difficult to find, just like the perfect altar wine *Malvaxia Sincerum*. That wine, not currently being marketed, remains more a "point of reference" for other Mass-wine producers. And indeed, the laudable characteristics of the perfect eucharistic minister described here are points of reference for our own ministry, an ideal to aim at. Liturgical ministry is something we grow into, something we shape ourselves into as it shapes us. Such ministry is not something that comes to us ready made, once and for all. Like a fine wine, our ministry is brought to perfection over time, enriched by experience, and savored as a source of joy in the Lord.

There won't be any international competition for the perfect eucharistic minister as there was for the perfect altar wine. The perfect eucharistic minister wouldn't want or need such a mark of honor. Such a minister knows that the call to minister the Body and Blood of Christ is a gift from God. To exercise the ministry of Communion humbly, faithfully, and generously is its own reward, a reward beyond price. It is one of God's ways of shaping us into the likeness of Jesus Christ, whose self-giving unto death remains the pattern for our own.

Notes

[1] Instruction *Immensae Caritatis* on Facilitating Sacramental Eucharistic Communion in Particular Circumstances, in *Vatican Council II: The Conciliar and Post Conciliar Documents*, ed. Austin Flannery, O.P. (Collegeville: The Liturgical Press, 1975) 226–27.

[2] Ibid., 227.

[3] Ibid.

[4] Augustine, Sermon 229 "On the Sacraments of the Faithful," trans. Sr. Mary Sarah Muldowney, R.S.M., in the Fathers of the Church series, vol. 38 (New York: The Fathers of the Church, Inc. 1959) 201.

[5] Roger Lloyd, *The Letters of Luke the Physician* (London: Allen & Unwin, Ltd., 1957) 72.

[6] Augustine, Sermon 229, 202.

[7] Ibid.

[8] From *Gather to Remember*, G.I.A. Publications, Inc., Copyright © 1982 by David Haas. Published and distributed by Cooperative Ministries, Washington, D.C., G.I.A. License 1332.

[9] "Order for the Commissioning of Extraordinary Ministers of Holy Communion," *Book of Blessings* (Collegeville: The Liturgical Press, 1989) no. 1875.

[10] Aidan Kavanagh, *Elements of Rite: A Handbook of Liturgical Style* (New York: Pueblo Publishing Company, Inc., 1982) 12.

[11] Augustine, Sermon 304, 1–4, in *The Liturgy of the Hours*, IV (New York: Catholic Book Publishing Co., 1975) 1305–1306.

[12] Augustine, Sermon 272, quoted in *Assembly*, the journal of the Notre Dame Center for Pastoral Liturgy, vol. 7, no. 3 (February 1981) 119.

[13] Bishops' Committee on the Liturgy, *Christian Commitment* (Washington, D.C.: United States Catholic Conference, 1978) n.p.

[14] *General Instruction of the Roman Missal,* 3rd typical ed. (International Commission on English in the Liturgy, 2002) no. 339.

[15] "Rite of Distributing Holy Communion by a Special Minister," no. 13, *The Rites of the Catholic Church*, II (New York: Pueblo Publishing Company, Inc., 1980) 169.

[16] Bishops' Committee on the Liturgy *Newsletter*, XII (August 1976) 30.

17 My reflection on Communion cups was published originally in *Assembly*, vol. 8, no. 1 (September 1981) 143.

18 Bishops' Committee on the Liturgy, *Study Text I: Holy Communion* (Washington, D.C.: United States Catholic Conference, 1973) 15.

19 Romano Guardini, *Sacred Signs*, trans. Grace Branham (Wilmington, Del.: Michael Glazier, Inc. 1979) 15.

20 Michael Ahlstrom, *Liturgy 80*, vol. 14, no. 1 (January–February 1983) 12.

21 Gabe Huck, "The Acolyte: Ministers of Communion," *Liturgy with Style and Grace* (Chicago: Liturgy Training Program, Archdiocese of Chicago, 1978) 110.

22 Instruction *Inaestimablile Donum* on Certain Norms Concerning Worship of the Eucharistic Mystery, no. 13.

23 Kenneth Untener, *Sunday Liturgy Can Be Better!* (Cincinnati: St. Anthony Messenger Press, 1980) 75.

24 Odo Casel, *The Mystery of Christian Worship*, ed. Burkhard Neunheuser, O.S.B. (Westminister, Md.: The Newman Press, 1962) 93.

25 Melissa Kay, "For Ministers of Communion," in *Touchstones for Liturgical Ministers*, ed. Virginia Sloyan (Washington, D.C.: The Liturgical Conference, 1978) 22.

26 Holy Communion and Worship of the Eucharist Outside Mass, no. 20, *The Rites of the Catholic Church*, I (New York: Pueblo Publishing Company, Inc., 1976) 462.

27 *Code of Canon Law: Latin-English Edition*, trans. prepared under the auspices of the Canon Law Society of America (Washington, D.C.: Canon Law Society of America, 1983) 343.

28 Constitution *Sacrosanctum Concilium* on the Sacred Liturgy, no. 35, in *Vatican Council II: The Conciliar and Post Conciliar Documents*, ed. Austin Flannery, O.P. (Collegeville: The Liturgical Press, 1975) 12.

Act of Personal Recommitment for Extraordinary Ministers of Holy Communion
(Based on the Rite of Commissioning)

I remember with gratitude that I have been entrusted with ministering the Eucharist, with taking Communion to the sick, and with giving it as Viaticum to the dying.

I have accepted the responsibility of being an example of Christian living in faith and conduct. I reaffirm my desire to strive for greater holiness through this sacrament of unity and love. I remember that, though many, we are one body because we share the one bread and the one cup.

I acknowledge that the ministry of Holy Communion requires me to be especially observant of the Lord's command to love my neighbor. For when he gave his Body and Blood as food to his disciples, he said to them: "This is my commandment, that you should love one another as I have loved you."

I again resolve to undertake the office of giving the Body and Blood of the Lord to my brothers and sisters, and so serve to build up the Church.

I again resolve to minister the Holy Eucharist with the utmost care and reverence.

I ask almighty God, the Father, the Son, ✠ and the Holy Spirit, to bless me as I give the bread of life and the cup of salvation to God's people, my brothers and sisters in the Lord. Strengthened by this sacrament, may we come at last to the banquet of heaven, where Jesus is Lord for ever and ever. Amen.